Who is a Next of Kin

John Ogbole

Table of content

Chapter 1: The origination of Next of Kin

- Exploring the concept of next of kin
- The significance of family ties
- Scriptures: "Behold, children are a heritage from the Lord, the fruit of the womb a reward." - Psalm 127:3

Chapter 2: Tracing Our Roots

- Discovering our familial heritage
- Genealogy and its importance
- Scriptures: "Honor your father and your mother, that your days may be long in the land that the Lord your God is giving you." - Exodus 20:12

Chapter 3: The Power of Family Bonds

- Understanding the strength of next of kin relationships
- Nurturing love and support within the family
- Scriptures: "Above all, keep loving one another earnestly, since love covers a multitude of sins." - 1 Peter 4:8

Chapter 4: Legal Aspects of Next of Kin

- Exploring the legal implications and rights of next of kin
- Responsibilities and decision-making authority

- Scriptures: "A good man leaves an inheritance to his children's children." - Proverbs 13:22

Chapter 5: Cultural Perspectives on Next of Kin

- Embracing diverse cultural views on family
- Unique practices and customs around the world
- Scriptures: "From one man he made all the nations, that they should inhabit the whole earth." - Acts 17:26

Chapter 6: Blended Families and Step-Relations

- Navigating complexities in modern family structures
- Building bridges and fostering harmony
- Scriptures: "Therefore a man shall leave his father and his mother and hold fast to his wife, and they shall become one flesh." - Genesis 2:24

Chapter 7: Next of Kin and Inheritance Laws

- Understanding inheritance laws and their impact
- Estate planning and avoiding conflicts
- Scriptures: "For where your treasure is, there your heart will be also." - Matthew 6:21

Chapter 8: Supporting Next of Kin in Times of Crisis

- Offering emotional and practical support during difficult times
- Strengthening bonds in moments of adversity

- Scriptures: "Bear one another's burdens, and so fulfill the law of Christ." - Galatians 6:2

Chapter 9: Next of Kin in the Modern World

- Exploring the evolving role of next of kin in contemporary society
- Balancing tradition with societal changes
- Scriptures: "And if it is evil in your eyes to serve the Lord, choose this day whom you will serve, whether the gods your fathers served in the region beyond the River, or the gods of the Amorites in whose land you dwell. But as for me and my house, we will serve the Lord." - Joshua 24:15

Chapter 10: Strengthening the Next of Kin Connection

- Practical tips for fostering strong family relationships
- Effective communication and resolving conflicts
- Scriptures: "And above all these put on love, which binds everything together in perfect harmony." - Colossians 3:14

Chapter 11: Who is a Next of Kin

- Spiritual View and Physical View: Understanding the Difference

This book is dedicated to men and women, young and old people who have past through challenge of been a next of kin and might have suffer pains of trying to carry the load of stress has a next of kin to family members that never believed in the ability of the next of kin chosen by the deceased or family leader etc. why the dedication? The writer of this book have experience a lot, with that experience that i wrote this book who is a next of kin to express it well to people and readers who a next of kin is, the important of a next of kin and value that is to be to a next of kin both old and young. To this end I dedicate this book to all next of kin that love do great things and impact in their world thank you.

Introduction

In the intricate tapestry of life, there exists a sacred thread that binds us all together—the unbreakable bonds of family. Our families, with their unique dynamics and deep-rooted connections, shape our identities and lay the foundation for our journey through this world. Within the realm of family, there exists a concept that holds profound significance—next of kin.

"Who is a Next of Kin: Embracing the Bonds of Family" delves into the captivating realm of next of kin, inviting you on a transformative exploration of the ties that bind us. Through this captivating journey, we will navigate the intricacies of familial relationships, unravel the rich tapestry of heritage, and uncover the power and responsibilities bestowed upon those entrusted with the mantle of next of kin.

As we embark on this remarkable expedition, we draw inspiration from the words of the Scriptures, for they hold timeless wisdom that resonates across generations. The

Scriptures remind us of the importance of family, urging us to honor and cherish the gifts that it bestows upon us. In their pages, we find solace, guidance, and encouragement to navigate the complexities of next of kin relationships.

"For where your treasure is, there your heart will be also." (Matthew 6:21)

With these compelling words, the Scriptures remind us that our true treasure lies within the realm of family. It is within these precious bonds that our hearts find solace, love, and belonging. The concept of next of kin encapsulates the depth of these connections—a role that carries with it profound responsibilities and privileges.

Throughout the chapters of this book, we will embark on an enlightening journey, exploring the historical, cultural, and legal aspects of next of kin. We will traverse the terrain of blended families, delve into the intricacies of inheritance laws, and navigate the complexities of supporting our loved ones during times of crisis. Together, we will discover how to strengthen the next of kin connection, fostering harmonious relationships that withstand the tests of time.

As you embark on this profound exploration, may the words of the Scriptures resonate within your heart, guiding you on this transformative voyage. Let us embrace the beauty and significance of family ties, honoring the heritage that flows through our veins and celebrating the role of next of kin with reverence and love.

"For where two or three are gathered in my name, there am I among them." (Matthew 18:20)

Within the pages of this book, let us gather as a community of seekers, united by the desire to understand and appreciate the essence of next of kin. Together, let us embark on this enlightening journey, guided by the power of the Scriptures and fueled by the universal yearning for love, connection, and the unbreakable bonds of family.

Chapter 1

The origination of a next of Kin: In brief of understanding

In our everyday world, the phrase "next of kin" is familiar — a line found in hospital forms, legal documents, wills, or emergency contact sheets. But beyond its administrative use lies a powerful ancient origin, deeply rooted in biblical covenant, Hebrew law, and Greek understanding of family lineage. The term does not merely signify a relative — it embodies a spiritual responsibility, a legal right, and a sacred duty passed down through generations.

Understanding the origin of the next of kin brings fresh revelation to the value of family, inheritance, protection, and redemption. This chapter will guide you into the deeper meaning of the term, tracing its journey from biblical Hebrew and Greek words, to its powerful role in scripture and society.

1. More Than a Relative: What Next of Kin Means

Today, the "next of kin" refers to someone's closest living relative. This person:

- Makes decisions when someone is incapacitated,

- May inherit the estate of the deceased in the absence of a will,

- Often becomes the legal guardian of minor children,

- Acts on behalf of the family in sensitive or tragic times.

But biblically and historically, the next of kin was far more than a contact or heir — it was a person with divinely recognized roles: to protect, redeem, and uphold the legacy of the family.

2. The Hebrew Concept: *Go'el* (גָּאַל)

In Hebrew culture, the most equivalent term to "next of kin" is Go'el, often translated as kinsman-redeemer.

Meaning of Go'el:

From the root word *ga'al*, meaning "to redeem, to act as protector or rescuer."

The Go'el had four major duties in ancient Israel:

1. Redeem Property

    If a family member sold land due to poverty, the Go'el would buy it back to keep it within the family (Leviticus 25:25).

2. Redeem a Person from Slavery

    If a relative sold themselves into slavery, the Go'el had the right to buy their freedom (Leviticus 25:47–49).

3. Avenge Bloodshed

    Known as the "avenger of blood" (*go'el ha-dam*), he ensured justice for the killing of a relative (Numbers 35:19).

4. Preserve the Family Line

    In the case of a man who died without children, the Go'el

(typically the brother or close male relative) would marry the widow to produce offspring in his name (Deuteronomy 25:5-10).

> *"The nearest kinsman said, I may not redeem it for myself... Then said Boaz, What day thou buyest the field of the hand of Naomi, thou must buy it also of Ruth... to raise up the name of the dead upon his inheritance."*
> — Ruth 4:6, 5 (KJV)

The story of Ruth and Boaz is the most beautiful biblical example of this. Boaz acted as a next of kin, stepping into a redemptive role that restored the lineage of Ruth's deceased husband. He did not just inherit — he redeemed, loved, and gave life to a future generation.

3. The Greek Word: *Syggenēs* (συγγενής)

In the Greek language, especially in the New Testament, the term used for kin or relative is syggenēs (συγγενής).

- Root meaning: from *syn* (together) + *genos* (family, race).

- It means "of the same family, kin, or bloodline."

Jesus used this term when teaching about spiritual and physical family:

> "For whosoever shall do the will of God, the same is my brother, and my sister, and mother." — Mark 3:35

In Luke 1:58, when Elizabeth gave birth to John the Baptist:

> "And her neighbours and her cousins (syggenēs) heard how the Lord had shewed great mercy upon her…"

In Greek culture, kinship was primarily biological and social, determining inheritance, family honor, and care for elders. Yet in the gospel, Jesus elevated the idea of kinship from the natural to the spiritual — based on obedience to God.

4. From Language to Legacy: The English Evolution

The English phrase "next of kin" comes from Middle English and Old English origins.

- "Next": meaning nearest in line or position.

- "Kin": from *cynn* (Old English), meaning race, tribe, or family.

By the 14th century, the phrase came to refer to the nearest relative by blood or marriage. But while English usage made it sound administrative, its biblical and ancient roots give it great weight.

To be someone's next of kin is not simply a matter of name on a form — it is to be their protector, redeemer, witness, and legacy bearer.

5. The Redeeming Power of Kinship

Throughout scripture, God Himself reveals His character using the language of kinship and redemption. In Hosea 13:14, God says:

> *"I will ransom them from the power of the grave; I will redeem them from death…"*

Here, God acts as the ultimate Go'el, the one who saves His people not only from physical bondage but also from eternal separation.

And in Jesus Christ, God took on flesh to become our kinsman, sharing in our human nature so that He could legally and spiritually redeem us.

> *"Forasmuch then as the children are partakers of flesh and blood, he also himself likewise took part of the same…"* — Hebrews 2:14

Jesus became our spiritual next of kin — our kinsman-redeemer — paying the ultimate price on the cross to restore us back to the Father.

6. What This Means for Us Today

In our families, communities, and churches, understanding the concept of "next of kin" should reshape how we see:

- Responsibility: Being kin means showing up, not just existing.

- Redemption: God uses family ties to restore and redeem.

- Legacy: You may be the one called to stand in the gap for a brother, sister, or child.

- Spiritual Kinship: Even beyond blood, we are called to be family in Christ, bearing one another's burdens.

The Weight of Being next of kin is more than a person on paper — it is a divine calling rooted in history, language, and scripture. From the Go'el of the Old Testament to the kinsman Christ in the New, this role has always pointed to something greater: a life of sacrificial love, generational responsibility, and faithful redemption.

When you consider who your next of kin is — or whom you are next of kin to — remember: you are stepping into a role defined by

God, shaped by the ancient past, and meaningful for eternal destiny.

As a whole this chapter embarks on a transformative journey to unveil the profound concept of next of kin—a concept that holds immense validity and unravels the intricate web of family ties. As we delve into the depths of this understanding, we encounter the power and significance that next of kin relationships carry within the framework of our lives.

"We are all born into families, and our bonds with our relatives shape us, nurture us, and provide us with a sense of belonging."

From the very beginning, our lives are intertwined with those who share our bloodline. We are born into families, surrounded by the love, care, and guidance of our parents, grandparents, and siblings. These familial connections play a vital role in shaping our identities, molding our values, and instilling in us a sense of heritage. It is within the embrace of family that we find a safe haven—a place where we are accepted and cherished for who we are.

In our exploration of next of kin, we turn to the Scriptures for wisdom and understanding. Psalm 127:3 proclaims, "Behold, children are a heritage from the Lord, the fruit of the womb a reward." This verse encapsulates the divine nature of family ties, emphasizing that children are not merely a biological occurrence but a gift—an inheritance entrusted to us. It highlights the sacred responsibility we have as parents, siblings, and extended family members to nurture, guide, and protect the precious lives that have been bestowed upon us.

"Family is the cornerstone of society, the foundation upon which communities thrive."

As we continue our journey of unveiling the next of kin, we recognize that family extends beyond the immediate circle of relatives. It encompasses a broad spectrum of relationships, including grandparents, aunts, uncles, cousins, and even close family friends. These connections are not mere accidents of birth but intentional placements in our lives. They contribute to the richness of our familial tapestry, infusing it with diversity, support, and love.

The Scriptures affirm the importance of family ties and the role they play in our lives. Ephesians 2:19 reminds us, "So then you are no longer strangers and aliens, but you are fellow citizens with the saints and members of the household of God." This verse reminds us that as believers, we are part of a larger family—the family of God. It underscores the notion that our spiritual kinship transcends physical boundaries, uniting us in a bond of love and fellowship. In a real life today the next of kin comes out of a family and the family foundations from the beginning of both the father and the mother relationship to there children will determine the type of next of king that will be offer to represent the family in the society at large that is why foundation of a family members from daddy to mummy relationship which cover the love side, caring side, intimacy side and giving and receiving side of both parent and children to their wards play a vital role in create a good and best next of king that will save any situations. In the future starting from today. Any one chosen has a next of kin represent his or her family in the society at large, for he or she is a representer of that family, from that family, at that family, of his or her family world wide.

"But the true essence of next of kin extends beyond blood relations alone. It is the depth of connection, the unwavering love, and the commitment to one another that defines our familial bonds."

Next of kin relationships extend beyond genetics and biology. They encompass the bonds that are forged through shared experiences, mutual trust, and unconditional love. These connections often defy societal norms and conventional definitions, emphasizing the importance of chosen family—the individuals we hold dear, who support us in times of joy and adversity, and who stand by our side through thick and thin.

The Bible provides us with a powerful example of chosen family in the story of Ruth and Naomi. Ruth's commitment to Naomi, her mother-in-law, demonstrates the depth of their bond. In Ruth 1:16-17, she proclaims, "Where you go, I will go, and where you stay, I will stay. Your people will be my people, and your God my God." This profound declaration encapsulates the essence of next of kin relationships—the choice to stand by one another, to intertwine lives, and to create a bond that surpasses blood ties.

As we conclude this introductory chapter, let us reflect upon the profound words of Scripture. May we recognize the inherent value and sacredness of family ties—both biological and chosen. The unveiling of the next of kin concept allows us to appreciate the intricate web of connections that shape our lives, and it beckons us to embrace the responsibility, love, and support that come with being part of a family. Join us as we get deeper into the complexities of next of kin, exploring its historical, cultural, and legal dimensions. Together, we will navigate the tapestry of family, celebrating the bonds that bind us all. Next of kin is not what any man should take for granted but take serious because for any family not to lost is family heritage which is peculiar to all one must be conscious of the fact every one of us come from some where which is a family set up and a family set up is comprises of first generation to fourth generation like that like that till tenth generation. Your generation will continue if you have a next of kin as a family member, some people don't value next of kin but others do but the fact is next of kin is very important to life because anyhow living is dangerous no wonder the bible say a good man will alway live an inheritance for his children children **proverb 13:22** A good *man* leaveth an inheritance to his children's children: and the wealth of the sinner *is* laid up for the just.

And in the other setting a bad man or woman do not care about living inheritance that why at the end they will it their heritage to cat and dogs note that in the other hand some are rich but dont have anybody to share with. That is to tell you that there is power in having a next of kin, which start from you has a person next of kin is a transfer of authority and right to one person who is appointed and trusted spiritual and physically by the inheritor because nobody no tomorrow but God of all flesh in heaven. And everybody is an inheritor author by God grace and mercy but not everyone is an inheritor according to mans or woman power because it authority by will or by selection of trust and connection and collection this my child, boy, girl man or woman will not fail me or disappoint me even while i am gone to heaven or hell because nobody no the heart of man.

Chapter 2:

Tracing Our Roots: Discovering Our Familial Heritage

Every family have their own family heritage that need to be protected from value that will will suit the family, so therefore this chapter embarks on a journey of self-discovery, delving into the significance of tracing our roots and exploring our familial heritage. We will unravel the tapestry of our family history, exploring the profound impact it has on our identity, values, and sense of belonging.

"Every individual is woven into the fabric of their family's history, carrying within them the legacy of those who came before."

The study of genealogy and tracing our lineage is an opportunity to connect with our ancestors, to unravel the stories of their lives, and to honor the sacrifices they made. It is through understanding where we come from that we gain a deeper understanding of who we are. Exploring our familial heritage empowers us to embrace our cultural roots, traditions, and values, enriching our lives and shaping our worldview.

In the Scriptures, we find guidance and affirmation of the importance of honoring our family ties. Exodus 20:12 commands, "Honor your father and your mother, that your days may be long in the land that the Lord your God is giving you." This verse not only emphasizes the duty of children to respect and honor their parents, but it also highlights the significance of the intergenerational connection. It speaks to the idea that our familial heritage is a gift—a legacy that shapes our lives and impacts our future.

"The act of tracing our roots enables us to recognize the resilience, strength, and wisdom of those who came before us."

Genealogy not only allows us to trace our ancestral lineage but also helps us to understand the historical context in which our families lived. It offers a window into the challenges and triumphs they faced, the traditions they upheld, and the values they cherished. Through this exploration, we gain a profound appreciation for the resilience, strength, and wisdom of our forebears, realizing that their experiences have shaped and influenced who we have become.

As we delve into the depths of our familial heritage, we come to understand that our stories are interconnected. Each generation adds a thread to the tapestry, weaving a narrative that spans time and space. We are not isolated individuals but rather part of a broader narrative—an ongoing story of resilience, love, and the human experience.

"By embracing our familial heritage, we forge a stronger sense of identity and belonging."

Scripture reminds us of the importance of understanding our familial heritage and the impact it has on our lives. Proverbs 13:22 states, "A good man leaves an inheritance to his children's children." This verse emphasizes the legacy we inherit from our ancestors—their wisdom, values, and material possessions. By acknowledging and embracing this inheritance, we forge a stronger sense of identity and belonging, enabling us to navigate the complexities of life with a solid foundation.

Tracing our roots and discovering our familial heritage is not merely an intellectual exercise or a nostalgic journey. It is a powerful tool for personal growth and self-reflection. It invites us to honor and celebrate the resilience, sacrifices, and achievements of our ancestors while recognizing the interconnectedness of our lives with theirs.

"As we explore our familial heritage, we gain a greater appreciation for the diversity and richness of our human family."

The act of tracing our roots also opens our eyes to the broader human family. It allows us to discover connections to individuals from diverse backgrounds, cultures, and traditions. This realization fosters a sense of empathy, respect, and appreciation for the diversity that exists within our global community.

In this chapter, we have embarked on a journey to trace our roots, unravel our familial heritage, and embrace the significance of genealogy. Through Scriptures such as Exodus 20:12 and Proverbs 13:22, we have gained a deeper understanding of the importance of honoring our ancestors, acknowledging the inheritance we have received, and forging a stronger sense of identity and belonging.

As we continue our exploration, let us delve deeper into the richness of our familial heritage, uncovering the stories, traditions, and values that have shaped us. By tracing our roots, we connect with the tapestry of our past, fostering a deeper appreciation for the diverse and interconnected nature of our human family.

Chapter 3:

The Power of Family Bonds: Understanding the Strength of Next of Kin Relationships

In this chapter, I will talking about the profound power of family bonds and delve into the significance of next of kin relationships, to unravel the intricate web of love, support, and connection that exists within the family unit, recognizing its transformative impact on our lives.

"At the core of every strong family lies the foundation of love and support."

Family bonds are built on the pillars of love and support. They provide us with a sense of belonging, acceptance, and security. Within the embrace of our next of kin, we find a sanctuary where we can freely express ourselves, share our joys and sorrows, and seek solace during challenging times. These relationships shape our emotional well-being and contribute to our overall happiness and fulfillment.

The Scriptures remind us of the importance of nurturing love and support within the family. 1 Peter 4:8 declares, "Above all, keep loving one another earnestly, since love covers a multitude of sins." This verse speaks to the power of love as a unifying force within the family. It encourages us to cultivate a genuine, selfless love that transcends our flaws and shortcomings. By embracing this love, we create an environment where forgiveness, understanding, and compassion flourish, fostering deep and meaningful connections.

"Next of kin relationships provide a support system that accompanies us through the journey of life."

Our next of kin, whether parents, siblings, or extended family, form an unwavering support system that accompanies us through the ups and downs of life. They celebrate our successes, lend a listening ear during times of struggle, and offer guidance and wisdom gained from their own experiences. The strength of these relationships lies in their unconditional nature, where love is not based on achievement or perfection but on a genuine care for one another's well-being.

The Scriptures reinforce the importance of support and encouragement within the family. Galatians 6:2 instructs us, "Bear one another's burdens, and so fulfill the law of Christ." This verse calls us to stand by our next of kin, offering a helping hand and a compassionate heart. It emphasizes the transformative power of empathy and the responsibility we have to lift one another up during challenging times.

"Through the power of family bonds, we learn valuable life lessons and build a strong foundation for the future."

Next of kin relationships provide us with a fertile ground for personal growth and learning. Within our family units, we acquire life skills, values, and beliefs that shape our character and influence our choices. We learn the importance of respect, compromise, and communication, laying the groundwork for healthy relationships and successful interactions beyond the family sphere.

The Scriptures guide us in nurturing these qualities within the family context. Colossians 3:13 encourages us, "Bear with each other and forgive one another if any of you has a grievance against someone. Forgive as the Lord forgave you." This verse emphasizes the transformative power of forgiveness and highlights the importance of cultivating an atmosphere of grace and reconciliation within the family. By embodying forgiveness and grace, we lay the foundation for resilient and harmonious relationships.

In summary, next of kin relationships hold immense power and strength. Through love, support, and nurturing, we create a strong familial bond that uplifts us and shapes our lives. Scriptures such as 1 Peter 4:8 and Galatians 6:2 remind us of the significance of cultivating love, support, and empathy within the family. By embracing these principles, we foster an environment where we can learn, grow, and thrive together, creating a legacy of love that transcends generations.

The fact remains that the power of family bond will alway strengthen the next of kin that is choosing to do the job of a next of kin because the power that bond them to stand as one reading to any length for the next of kin that will be standing in the cap the rest of the family in all area as a people and family etc.

The power of family bonds lies in the deep love, support, and connection shared among relatives. Family bonds provide a sense of belonging, acceptance, and security. They are a source of comfort and strength during both joyful and challenging times. For example, when a family member faces a difficult situation, the rest of the family comes together to offer encouragement and assistance. These bonds nurture our emotional well-being and contribute to our overall happiness and fulfillment. Family bonds create a support system that accompanies us throughout life's journey, offering unwavering care, guidance, and wisdom. They teach us important life lessons, shape our character, and provide a strong foundation for future relationships. In essence, family bonds are a source of love, support, and resilience that enrich our lives and leave a lasting impact on our well-being.

One biblical example that illustrates the power of family bonds is the story of Joseph and his brothers in the book of Genesis. Despite the hardships and conflicts they faced, the bond of family ultimately prevailed. Joseph's brothers initially betrayed him, selling him into slavery out of jealousy. However, years later, during a time of famine, Joseph's brothers came to Egypt seeking food. When Joseph revealed his identity to them, instead of seeking revenge, he showed forgiveness and embraced his family with love and compassion. This powerful display of family bonds transformed their relationships, leading to reconciliation and the preservation of their lineage.

This story highlights the enduring strength of family bonds. Despite the trials and tribulations they may face, families have the potential to heal, forgive, and support one another. It serves as a reminder that even in challenging circumstances, the power of love and forgiveness can overcome adversity and restore the harmony within a family.

Chapter 4:

Legal Aspects of Next of Kin: Exploring Rights, Responsibilities, and Decision-Making Authority

In this chapter, we are looking into the legal implications of being a next of kin, which will be exploring the rights, responsibilities, and decision-making authority that come with this role. Understanding the legal aspects is crucial in navigating the complexities of family dynamics and ensuring the well-being of our loved ones.

"Being a next of kin involves both privileges and responsibilities, as it carries with it legal implications."

As a next of kin, you are often bestowed with certain legal rights and responsibilities. These vary from one jurisdiction to another, but they typically include decision-making authority in matters such as healthcare, financial affairs, and guardianship. Being a next of kin means having the privilege of being entrusted with important decisions that impact the lives of your family members.

Proverbs 13:22 states, "A good man leaves an inheritance to his children's children." This verse emphasizes the responsibility of the next of kin to safeguard and manage the assets and legacy passed down through generations. It highlights the importance of acting in a responsible and just manner, ensuring the preservation and wise utilization of family resources.

"Next of kin hold a significant role in making important decisions for their family members."

Next of kin often play a vital role in making critical decisions on behalf of their family members, especially in situations where an individual may be incapacitated or unable to make decisions for themselves. This responsibility may involve choices related to healthcare treatment, financial matters, or even end-of-life decisions.

In the Scriptures, we find examples of individuals fulfilling this role of decision-maker. For instance, in the book of Genesis, Abraham acts as the next of kin for his son Isaac when he arranges for a suitable spouse for him. Abraham ensures that his son enters into a marriage that aligns with their faith and cultural values. This example highlights the important role of the next of kin in guiding and protecting the interests of their family members.

"Legal aspects of next of kin require a balance between autonomy and acting in the best interest of our loved ones."

While next of kin have decision-making authority, it is essential to strike a balance between respecting an individual's autonomy and acting in their best interests. This responsibility requires careful consideration and consultation with other family members, medical professionals, or legal advisors.

The Bible encourages us to seek wisdom and guidance in making decisions that affect our family members. Proverbs 15:22 advises, "Without counsel, plans fail, but with many advisers, they succeed." This verse emphasizes the importance of seeking input from others, acknowledging that wise decision-making often involves seeking counsel and considering multiple perspectives.

"In fulfilling our legal responsibilities as next of kin, we should prioritize the well-being and best interests of our loved ones."

Our legal responsibilities as next of kin extend beyond decision-making authority. They also involve ensuring the well-being and best interests of our family members. This may include providing emotional support, advocating for their rights, and safeguarding their welfare.

The Scriptures guide us in this aspect of our responsibilities. Galatians 5:13 reminds us, "You, my brothers and sisters, were called to be free. But do not use your freedom to indulge the flesh; rather, serve one another humbly in love." This verse underscores the importance of selfless service and love in fulfilling our role as next of kin. It calls us to prioritize the well-being of our loved ones, serving them with humility and compassion.

In conclusion, understanding the legal aspects of being a next of kin is crucial in fulfilling our rights, responsibilities, and decision-making authority. The Bible, through verses such as Proverbs 13:22 and Galatians 5:13, provides guidance and wisdom in navigating these legal implications. By striking a balance between autonomy and acting in the best interest of our loved ones, we can fulfill our roles as next of kin with integrity, compassion, and a commitment to their well-being.

Chapter 5:

Cultural Perspectives on Next of Kin

As our faces are different so there are diverse cultural perspectives on the concept of next of kin show how different our believes are, and to understand and value the roles and responsibilities associated with being a next of kin it depended on our culture value and foundational structure builded on because of different family pattern and ways of life . By examining these perspectives, we gain a deeper appreciation for the richness and significance of familial ties across various cultural backgrounds.

"Next of kin relationships are influenced by cultural beliefs, traditions, and values, shaping the roles and responsibilities within families."

Culture plays a profound role in shaping our understanding of next of kin relationships. It influences the roles, expectations, and obligations associated with being a next of kin. Cultural beliefs, traditions, and values guide our behaviors and interactions within the family unit.

Acts 17:26 states, "From one man he made all the nations, that they should inhabit the whole earth; and he marked out their appointed times in history and the boundaries of their lands." This verse reminds us of the diversity of cultures and the interconnectedness of all humanity. It emphasizes that our cultural backgrounds are part of God's design, contributing to the richness and beauty of our shared human experience.

"In some cultures, the concept of next of kin extends beyond immediate family members to include extended relatives and even close friends."

Different cultures have varying definitions of next of kin, with some cultures extending the concept beyond immediate family members. In certain societies, extended relatives, such as aunts, uncles, and cousins, hold a significant role as next of kin.

This broader understanding of next of kin expands the support network and reinforces the importance of maintaining strong bonds within the larger family unit.

An example from the Bible that reflects this cultural perspective is seen in the story of Ruth and Naomi (Ruth 1:16-17). After the death of their husbands, Naomi, as the mother-in-law, became Ruth's next of kin. Ruth, coming from a different cultural background as a Moabite, embraced Naomi as her own family, demonstrating the significance of extended kinship ties and the commitment to support and care for one another.

"Cultural perspectives on next of kin influence the roles and responsibilities within families."

Cultural perspectives on next of kin significantly impact the roles and responsibilities assigned to individuals within families. In some cultures, the next of kin may have specific duties such as caretaking, providing financial support, or preserving family traditions. These roles are deeply rooted in cultural norms and expectations, shaping the dynamics and structure of the family unit.

For instance, in many cultures, the eldest son holds a prominent role as the next of kin, responsible for upholding family traditions and carrying on the family name. This cultural perspective reflects the emphasis on lineage and continuity of family heritage.

"In conclusion, cultural perspectives on next of kin highlight the diverse ways in which familial ties are understood and valued."

Cultural perspectives on next of kin reveal the intricate tapestry of family relationships across different societies. They demonstrate how cultural beliefs, traditions, and values influence our understanding of roles, responsibilities, and obligations within the family. By appreciating these cultural perspectives, we gain a deeper understanding of the universal importance of next of kin relationships in fostering love, support, and connection.

By recognizing the diverse cultural perspectives on next of kin, we celebrate the beauty of our shared humanity and honor the rich tapestry of family ties that bind us together. Despite our cultural differences, we are united in the understanding that next of kin relationships are a vital cornerstone of our lives, offering support, guidance, and a sense of belonging.

Chapter 6:

Blended Families and Step-Relations: Navigating Complexities in Modern Family Structures, Building Bridges, and Fostering Harmony

The complexities arising in modern family structures, particularly in blended families and step-relations. Looking at the challenges faced by individuals who navigate these dynamics and discuss strategies for building bridges and fostering harmony within these unique family units. By drawing wisdom from relevant biblical texts and other sources, we aim to provide guidance and understanding to readers in similar situations.

Genesis 2:24 states, "Therefore a man shall leave his father and his mother and hold fast to his wife, and they shall become one flesh." This verse reminds us of the original design for marriage, highlighting the union of two individuals as they form a new family unit. However, in the context of blended families, this verse takes on an expanded meaning, emphasizing the importance of unity and commitment as new family structures are formed.

"Blended families and step-relations bring together individuals from different backgrounds, requiring understanding, patience, and open communication."

Blended families often consist of individuals who come from different backgrounds and have experienced previous relationships. This dynamic introduces unique challenges as new family members adjust to living together and forming relationships. It requires understanding, patience, and open communication to navigate the complexities that arise.

In the biblical narrative, we see the story of Joseph, who became a stepfather to Jesus. Joseph's journey involved accepting Mary as his wife and embracing Jesus as his own, despite not being his biological father. This example illustrates the importance of love, acceptance, and the willingness to build bridges within blended families and step-relations.

"Building bridges and fostering harmony in blended families requires intentional efforts, empathy, and mutual respect."

To foster harmony within blended families, intentional efforts must be made to build bridges and establish healthy relationships. This involves empathizing with one another's experiences, recognizing and validating emotions, and fostering an atmosphere of mutual respect. Open communication, compromise, and shared values play crucial roles in creating a strong foundation for blended families.

Ephesians 4:32 advises us to "Be kind to one another, tenderhearted, forgiving one another, as God in Christ forgave you." This biblical principle guides us in extending kindness, forgiveness, and understanding to our step-relations. It encourages us to prioritize compassion and empathy, nurturing an environment of love and support within blended families.

"Blended families have the opportunity to create a new, unique sense of unity and belonging."

Despite the complexities, blended families have the potential to create a new sense of unity and belonging. Through intentional efforts, family members can develop deep connections, establish traditions, and build a shared identity that encompasses the unique blend of backgrounds and experiences.

Romans 12:16 advises us to "Live in harmony with one another. Do not be haughty, but associate with the lowly. Never be wise in your own sight." This verse reminds us of the importance of humility and the willingness to embrace others, regardless of their background or role in the family. It encourages us to seek harmony and unity, fostering an environment where everyone feels valued and included.

"In conclusion, blended families and step-relations require understanding, empathy, and intentional efforts to build bridges and foster harmony."

Blended families and step-relations bring together individuals from different backgrounds, and navigating the complexities of these relationships requires understanding, empathy, and intentional efforts to build bridges and foster harmony. By drawing wisdom from biblical texts and embracing principles of love, acceptance, and forgiveness, blended families can create a strong sense of unity and belonging, enriching the lives of all family members involved.

By embracing the challenges and opportunities that come with blended families, individuals can grow in love, patience, and understanding. Together, they can create a supportive and nurturing environment that celebrates the uniqueness of each family member while forging strong bonds that withstand the complexities of modern family structures.

The story of Ruth and Naomi (Ruth 1:16-17): Ruth, a Moabite, became part of Naomi's family when she married Naomi's son. After Naomi's husband and sons passed away, Ruth chose to stay with Naomi, demonstrating a deep bond and commitment to her step-family.

The story of Joseph and Jesus (Matthew 1:18-25): Joseph, who became Jesus' stepfather, embraced Mary and accepted Jesus as his own, despite not being Jesus' biological father. Joseph's love, care, and guidance exemplify the role of a step-parent in nurturing and supporting a child.

The story of Esther and Mordecai (Esther 2:7, 15-18): Esther, an orphan, was raised by her cousin Mordecai. Mordecai took on the role of a step-parent, providing love, guidance, and protection for Esther. Their relationship showcases the strength of step-relations and the transformative impact they can have on a person's life.

These examples demonstrate the power of love, acceptance, and commitment in blended families and step-relations. They showcase the beauty that can emerge when individuals embrace and care for one another, regardless of biological ties.

Chapter 7:

Next of Kin and Inheritance Laws: Understanding the Impact, Estate Planning, and Conflict Avoidance

Looking at the realm of inheritance laws and their impact on next of kin relationships. the importance of understanding these laws, engaging in thoughtful estate planning, and fostering harmony among family members to avoid conflicts that may arise during the distribution of assets. By drawing wisdom from relevant biblical texts and examples, we aim to shed light on this critical aspect of family dynamics. Note all country in the world have practical laws that work around the world but some do have and it working it work of peace today in most family by the guidance we see if not destruction would have been the order of the day that God people are taking responsibility in most case but more has to be don to perfect this issues on ground that not all that are expressed but are dying without knowing.

Matthew 6:21 reminds us, "For where your treasure is, there your heart will be also." This verse speaks to the significance of our material possessions and the need to handle them with wisdom and care. In the context of inheritance, it encourages us to approach the subject with a balanced perspective, recognizing the importance of both material wealth and the well-being of our loved ones.

"Understanding inheritance laws is crucial for making informed decisions and preserving family relationships."

Inheritance laws can be complex and vary from one jurisdiction to another. It is crucial for individuals to have a basic understanding of these laws to make informed decisions regarding their estate and assets. By familiarizing themselves with legal requirements, individuals can ensure that their wishes are properly documented and their loved ones are protected.

An example of the importance of understanding inheritance laws can be seen in the story of the prodigal son (Luke 15:11-32). In this parable, the younger son demanded his share of the inheritance from his father prematurely, which resulted in conflict and strained relationships within the family. This story highlights the consequences of not considering the legal and familial implications of inheritance, emphasizing the need for thoughtful planning and communication.

"Estate planning is essential for ensuring the smooth transfer of assets and minimizing potential conflicts."

Estate planning involves making arrangements for the distribution of assets after one's passing. It includes creating a will, designating beneficiaries, and establishing trusts if necessary. Thoughtful estate planning not only ensures that one's wishes are carried out but also helps minimize potential conflicts among family members.

Proverbs 13:22 states, "A good man leaves an inheritance to his children's children." This verse encourages individuals to consider the long-term impact of their financial decisions. By engaging in effective estate planning, individuals can leave a lasting legacy that provides for future generations, fostering family unity and financial stability.

"Avoiding conflicts during the inheritance process requires open communication, transparency, and sensitivity."

Conflicts often arise during the inheritance process, leading to strained relationships and emotional distress. To avoid such conflicts, it is crucial to foster open communication, maintain transparency, and approach discussions with sensitivity. Family members should have opportunities to express their concerns, and efforts should be made to address any potential misunderstandings or disputes.

In the biblical narrative, we find the story of Abraham and Lot (Genesis 13:5-9). When conflicts arose over the distribution of land between their herdsmen, Abraham initiated open and peaceful communication with Lot to resolve the issue. This example highlights the importance of addressing conflicts promptly and seeking resolution in a spirit of understanding and cooperation.

"In conclusion, understanding inheritance laws, engaging in estate planning, and fostering open communication are vital for preserving family relationships and minimizing conflicts."

By understanding inheritance laws, engaging in thoughtful estate planning, and fostering open communication, individuals can navigate the complex terrain of inheritance while preserving family relationships. By aligning their financial decisions with biblical principles of wisdom, fairness, and love, they can ensure the smooth transfer of assets and promote harmony among their next of kin.

Ultimately, the inheritance process provides an opportunity to demonstrate love and respect for one's family members and to leave a lasting legacy that honors both their material well-being and their emotional and spiritual needs. Through careful planning and compassionate communication, families can navigate the complexities of inheritance with grace and unity.

In a practical example, imagine a family where there are differing expectations regarding the distribution of assets. Open communication becomes essential in such situations. By initiating honest and respectful conversations, family members can address their concerns, share their perspectives, and seek common ground. Through transparency and sensitivity to each other's needs and desires, conflicts can be minimized, fostering a harmonious environment for the next of kin.

In summary, next of kin and inheritance laws require careful consideration, planning, and compassionate communication. By aligning our financial decisions with biblical principles of wisdom, fairness, and love, we can navigate this complex terrain. Through a combination of legal knowledge and open dialogue, we can ensure that the inheritance process respects the wishes of the deceased, preserves family unity, and leaves a lasting legacy that reflects our values and priorities.

Chapter 8:

Supporting Next of Kin in Times of Crises: Offering Emotional and Practical Support During Difficult Times, Strengthening Bonds in Moments of Adversity

The importance of providing unwavering support to our next of kin during times of crises. the significance of offering both emotional and practical assistance, strengthening the bonds of love and unity even in the face of adversity will be expressed. Drawing inspiration from Galatians 6:2 and other relevant biblical texts, let's elaborate on this topic to provide valuable insights for the readers.

Galatians 6:2 reminds us, "Bear one another's burdens, and so fulfill the law of Christ." This verse encapsulates the essence of supporting our next of kin in times of crises. It calls us to embody empathy, compassion, and selflessness as we walk alongside our loved ones through their struggles.

"Supporting our next of kin during crises involves being there for them emotionally, providing a listening ear, and offering comfort."

During difficult times, our loved ones often need someone to lean on emotionally. We can offer a listening ear, allowing them to express their fears, frustrations, and sadness without judgment. Our presence and understanding can bring solace and reassurance, letting them know they are not alone in their struggles.

An example from the Bible is the story of Job. When Job faced unimaginable trials, his friends initially offered him support by sitting silently with him for seven days, sharing in his grief (Job 2:11-13). Their presence demonstrated the power of silent companionship, which can be a source of great comfort during times of crises.

"Practical support involves tangible acts of kindness and assistance to alleviate the burdens of our next of kin."

Practical support plays a vital role in easing the burdens faced by our loved ones. This can include providing meals, helping with household chores, offering financial assistance, or assisting with childcare. These acts of kindness demonstrate our commitment to walking alongside our next of kin during their challenging times.

In the New Testament, we find the story of the Good Samaritan (Luke 10:30-37). The Good Samaritan went beyond offering emotional support and provided practical aid to the injured man, tending to his wounds and providing for his care. This example highlights the importance of practical assistance in supporting others during their crises.

"In moments of adversity, our bonds with next of kin can grow stronger as we offer support and stand united."

Adversity has the potential to strengthen the bonds within families. When we rally together to support our next of kin during crises, it deepens our connection and fosters resilience. By demonstrating love, empathy, and unwavering support, we create an environment where our loved ones feel safe, valued, and uplifted.

The story of Ruth and Naomi exemplifies the power of unity and support in the face of adversity (Ruth 1:16-17). Despite facing tremendous challenges, Ruth remained committed to supporting her mother-in-law, Naomi. Their unwavering bond and mutual support ultimately led to their restoration and blessings.

In conclusion, supporting our next of kin in times of crises requires both emotional and practical assistance. By embodying the spirit of Galatians 6:2, we can bear one another's burdens and fulfill the law of Christ. By providing a listening ear, offering comfort, and extending practical help, we can strengthen the bonds of love and unity within our families. Just as biblical examples showcase the power of support, our commitment to our next of kin during their difficult times can bring comfort, healing, and growth to all involved.

"In our efforts to support our next of kin in times of crises, we can take our support to another level by providing spiritual nourishment and promoting resilience."

Spiritual support plays a crucial role in helping our loved ones navigate the storms of life. By offering words of encouragement, sharing uplifting scriptures, and praying together, we can provide a source of hope and strength. Our spiritual support reminds them of their connection to a higher power and helps them find solace in their faith.

For example, consider a family facing a health crisis. In addition to offering practical assistance and emotional support, they gather for prayer, seeking divine intervention and finding comfort in the assurance that they are not alone in their struggles. This collective spiritual support can instill a sense of peace and empower them to face the challenges with renewed strength.

Furthermore, promoting resilience within our next of kin is an invaluable aspect of support during crises. Resilience enables individuals to bounce back from adversity and find new ways to thrive. By encouraging them to develop coping strategies, fostering a growth mindset, and emphasizing the importance of self-care, we empower them to overcome their challenges and emerge stronger.

Drawing inspiration from 2 Corinthians 4:8-9, which states, "We are afflicted in every way, but not crushed; perplexed, but not driven to despair; persecuted, but not forsaken; struck down, but not destroyed," we can share this message of resilience and hope with our loved ones. By reminding them of the inherent strength they possess, we empower them to persevere through their crises and emerge victorious.

Consider a family facing financial hardships. In addition to offering practical support, they engage in discussions about budgeting, financial planning, and exploring new opportunities. By instilling a sense of resilience and providing them with tools to navigate their financial challenges, we equip them with the confidence to overcome their difficulties and create a brighter future.

In summary, supporting our next of kin in times of crises goes beyond emotional and practical assistance. By providing spiritual nourishment and promoting resilience, we elevate our support to another level. Through prayer, sharing scriptures, and emphasizing the power of faith, we offer a source of hope and strength. By encouraging resilience, fostering growth mindsets, and providing tools for coping, we empower our loved ones to overcome their challenges and find renewed purpose. Together, we can stand united and navigate the storms of life, fostering a bond of unwavering support that brings comfort, healing, and growth to our next of kin.

Chapter 9:

Next of Kin in the Modern World: Embracing the Changing Dynamics

the evolving dynamics of next of kin relationships in the modern world, brought about by changing family structures, geographical distances, and cultural shifts. Let's summarize this chapter by providing examples that illustrate the key points:

> Blended Families: In today's world, blended families have become increasingly common. Consider a scenario where two individuals with children from previous relationships come together to form a new family unit. Navigating the dynamics of step-parents, step-siblings, and biological children requires open communication, flexibility, and a willingness to embrace and integrate multiple family units. Long-Distance Relationships: With globalization and advancements in technology, families often find themselves living in different cities, countries, or even continents. Despite the physical distance, maintaining strong next of kin relationships is possible. For instance, regular video calls, shared online platforms for communication and updates, and making intentional

efforts to come together for important family events can help bridge the geographical gaps and foster a sense of connectedness.

Cultural Diversity: In our increasingly multicultural world, next of kin relationships can be influenced by diverse cultural backgrounds and practices. For example, in some cultures, extended family members play a significant role in the upbringing of children, sharing responsibilities and contributing to their overall well-being. Embracing and appreciating these cultural differences enhances the richness of next of kin relationships and strengthens family bonds.

Chosen Families: Beyond blood relations, the concept of chosen families has gained prominence. These are close-knit groups of individuals who may not be biologically related but share deep bonds of love, support, and commitment. This can include close friends, mentors, or individuals who have become like family through shared experiences and mutual care. Such chosen families demonstrate the capacity for building meaningful and supportive relationships outside traditional family structures.

LGBTQ+ Families: The modern world has seen significant progress in recognizing and celebrating diverse family structures, including LGBTQ+ families. Same-sex couples and their children form loving and supportive family units, challenging traditional notions of next of kin relationships. By embracing and affirming the validity and importance of these families, society can foster inclusivity and create a nurturing environment for all individuals to thrive.

Single-Parent Families: Single-parent families are another prominent feature of the modern world. Whether by choice or circumstances, single parents take on the role of both parents, providing emotional, financial, and practical support to their children. These families exemplify resilience and demonstrate the strength of the next of kin relationship between a single parent and their child.

In summary, the modern world presents us with diverse next of kin relationships that go beyond traditional structures. Blended families, long-distance relationships, cultural diversity, chosen families, LGBTQ+ families, and single-parent families all offer unique examples of how next of kin relationships can adapt and flourish in the modern era. By embracing these changing dynamics, fostering open communication, and recognizing the value of all types of family connections, we can build strong, supportive, and inclusive next of kin relationships that transcend societal expectations and nurture the well-being of al involved.

Chapter 10:

Strengthening the Next of Kin Connection: Practical Tips for Fostering Strong Family Relationships, Effective Communication, and Resolving Conflicts

This chapter will practical strategies for strengthening the next of kin connection and nurturing strong family relationship to express, the importance of effective communication, conflict resolution, and the power of love and forgiveness. Drawing inspiration from Colossians 3:14 and other relevant biblical texts, let's expand on these concepts and widen the scope of the chapter to provide a deeper understanding for the readers.

Colossians 3:14 reminds us, "And over all these virtues put on love, which binds them all together in perfect unity." This verse encapsulates the foundation of fostering strong family relationships—love. Love serves as the catalyst for effective communication, conflict resolution, and building lasting connections within our next of kin.

Effective Communication: Communication forms the cornerstone of healthy family relationships. By actively listening, expressing ourselves honestly and respectfully, and seeking to understand one another's perspectives, we create an environment of open dialogue. Proverbs 18:13 urges us, "To answer before listening—that is folly and shame." Taking the time to truly listen to one another without interruption fosters understanding and strengthens the bonds of connection.

Conflict Resolution: Conflicts are a natural part of any relationship, including within families. The key lies in resolving conflicts in a constructive and loving manner. Ephesians 4:26 advises, "In your anger do not sin: Do not let the sun go down while you are still angry." Promptly addressing conflicts and finding mutually beneficial solutions prevents unresolved issues from festering and damaging the next of kin connection. Active problem-solving, empathy, and a willingness to seek compromise contribute to healthier and more harmonious family dynamics.

Love and Forgiveness: Love and forgiveness are essential components of building and maintaining strong family relationships. 1 Corinthians 13:7 teaches us that love "always protects, always trusts, always hopes, always perseveres." By demonstrating acts of kindness, expressing appreciation, and extending forgiveness when necessary, we create an atmosphere of acceptance, understanding, and grace. These acts of love and forgiveness nurture emotional bonds and help heal wounds, strengthening the fabric of the next of kin connection.

Quality Time: Setting aside dedicated time for shared activities and meaningful conversations strengthens family bonds. Whether it's engaging in hobbies together, planning family outings, or simply gathering around the dinner table for regular meals, quality time fosters a sense of belonging and creates lasting memories. Psalm 133:1 reminds us, "How good and pleasant it is when God's people live together in unity." By intentionally investing time in one another, we create opportunities for deeper connection and intimacy.

Cultivating Respect and Empathy: Respect and empathy are foundational for building strong family relationships. Recognizing and valuing each family member's individuality, perspectives, and contributions promotes a culture of mutual respect. Philippians 2:3-4 exhorts us, "Do nothing out of selfish ambition or vain conceit. Rather, in humility value others above yourselves, not looking to your own interests but each of you to the interests of the others." By cultivating empathy and considering the feelings and needs of others, we create an environment of trust, understanding, and support.

In conclusion, fostering strong next of kin connections requires intentional effort and a commitment to love, effective communication, conflict resolution, and forgiveness. By embodying the virtues of Colossians 3:14 and drawing wisdom from biblical texts, we can navigate the complexities of family relationships with grace and understanding. As we prioritize love, practice effective communication, resolve conflicts in healthy ways, and cultivate respect and empathy, we strengthen the bonds that hold our families together, creating a legacy of love, unity, and harmony for generations to come.

strengthening next of kin connections in today's world, along with relevant Bible examples that resonate with our contemporary society:

> Embracing Technology: In today's digital age, technology can be utilized to bridge the gap between family members who are physically distant. Video calls, social media platforms, and messaging apps enable regular communication, sharing of updates, and even virtual family gatherings. Just as the apostle Paul used letters to communicate and stay connected with early Christian

communities (e.g., 1 Corinthians 5:9), we can leverage technology to foster meaningful connections with our next of kin, transcending geographical boundaries.

Balancing Individuality and Togetherness: Modern society places a strong emphasis on individuality, which can sometimes lead to a neglect of familial bonds. However, the Bible teaches us the importance of honoring our family relationships. Jesus himself, while ministering to the masses, also prioritized spending time with his disciples and his earthly family (Mark 3:31-35). We can learn from this example by finding a balance between pursuing personal goals and investing in the unity and strength of our next of kin connections.

Nurturing Intergenerational Relationships: In today's fast-paced world, intergenerational relationships are often overlooked. However, the Bible encourages the passing down of wisdom from one generation to the next. Just as Paul advised Timothy based on his own experiences (2 Timothy 3:10-11), we can seek guidance and mentorship from older family members, while also imparting our own wisdom to the younger ones. This intergenerational exchange enriches our family connections and promotes growth and understanding across different age groups.

Overcoming Cultural Barriers: Contemporary society is characterized by diverse cultures and backgrounds. When next of kin relationships cross cultural boundaries, it is essential to embrace and respect each other's traditions and customs. The early church faced similar challenges, with people from different cultures and backgrounds coming together as one body in Christ (Galatians 3:28). By recognizing and appreciating the uniqueness of each cultural heritage within our next of kin connections, we foster a deeper sense of unity and mutual respect.

Prioritizing Quality Time: Busy schedules and numerous commitments can strain family relationships. However, carving out intentional quality time is vital for nurturing next of kin connections. Jesus modeled this by prioritizing spending meaningful time with his disciples, even amid his demanding ministry (Luke 10:38-42). By setting aside distractions, being present, and engaging in activities that promote bonding and shared experiences, we create lasting memories and strengthen the ties that bind us as a family.

Extending Grace and Forgiveness: In our imperfect human interactions, conflicts and misunderstandings are bound to arise. However, the Bible calls us to extend grace and practice forgiveness within our next of kin connections. Just as Joseph forgave his brothers who had sold him into slavery (Genesis 50:15-21), we can seek reconciliation and healing, letting go of past hurts and embracing a future filled with love and unity.

By incorporating these principles into our modern lives, we can enhance the strength and depth of our next of kin connections. As we embrace technology, balance individuality with togetherness, nurture intergenerational relationships, overcome cultural barriers, prioritize quality time, and extend grace and forgiveness, we create a foundation of love, unity, and harmony within our families that aligns with the timeless teachings of the Bible.

Chapter 11:

Who is a Next of Kin - Spiritual View and Physical View: Understanding the Difference

In this chapter, The who is a next of kin has two dimensions to i from my area of understanding, revelation, insight and view point from experience in life and in my work and deeds also. The spiritual aspect is the revelation of who we are in christ and what God has put in us and around us and what he has show to us to the via is power and word has we connect spiritually to hear and see his promises and do his covenants to change our status quo into reality manifesting physically for the world to see now and how far we have has the king and priest he has made us through is word that we believed which bring the spirit to play in the physical no workings of the words we hear and see there never be a physical performance of the spiritual this he has show us from the mirror of his word Gods words which tested and trusted through fire to bring any man breakthrough, deli

> Spiritual View: From a spiritual perspective, the next of kin relationship transcends blood ties and extends to our connection with God and the wider spiritual family. In this view, we recognize that all human beings are created in the image of God (Genesis 1:27) and are part of the larger family of believers through faith in Jesus Christ (Galatians 3:26). This spiritual kinship emphasizes the unity, love, and shared identity we have as children of God, regardless of our biological relationships.

The spiritual view acknowledges that our ultimate next of kin is God Himself. Jesus spoke of this spiritual connection when He said, "Whoever does God's will is my brother and sister and mother" (Mark 3:35). In this sense, our spiritual next of kin includes fellow believers who share a common faith and commitment to following God's will. It emphasizes the importance of nurturing and supporting one another in our spiritual journey.

> Physical View: The physical view of next of kin pertains to our biological or legal family relationships. It focuses on

the immediate and extended family members who are connected through blood ties, marriage, or legal bonds. This includes parents, siblings, children, and other relatives who share a familial connection based on birth or legal recognition.

The physical view of next of kin emphasizes the roles and responsibilities associated with biological and legal ties. It encompasses matters such as inheritance, legal guardianship, medical decision-making, and familial obligations. This view recognizes the importance of maintaining and cherishing these relationships, as they form the foundation of our immediate support system and societal structure.

While the physical view of next of kin is based on earthly relationships, the spiritual view acknowledges the deeper spiritual bond we share as believers in God. It transcends the limitations of biology and legal ties, emphasizing the eternal significance of our connection with God and fellow believers.

It is essential to note that both the spiritual and physical views of next of kin are significant and complement each other. While the physical view addresses our earthly responsibilities and relationships, the spiritual view highlights our ultimate connection to God and the wider spiritual family. Balancing and honoring both perspectives allows us to navigate the complexities of family dynamics while recognizing the profound spiritual dimension of our next of kin relationships.

In conclusion, understanding the difference between the spiritual and physical views of next of kin provides a holistic perspective on familial relationships. While the physical view focuses on biological and legal ties, the spiritual view recognizes our connection to God and fellow believers. By embracing both perspectives, we can nurture and strengthen our earthly family bonds while also cultivating a deeper spiritual kinship rooted in faith and shared devotion to God.

> Spiritual View: The spiritual view of next of kin goes beyond biological or legal relationships and encompasses our connection with God and fellow believers. It recognizes that we are all created in the image of God and acknowledges the spiritual bond we share as part of the

larger family of believers. This view emphasizes the spiritual unity, love, and shared identity we have as children of God.

In simpler terms, the spiritual view tells us that our next of kin extends beyond just our immediate family members. It includes those who share the same faith and commitment to following God's teachings. So, while we may have family members by blood or law, our spiritual next of kin also includes people who believe in and follow God, forming a larger spiritual family.

> Physical View: The physical view of next of kin focuses on our biological or legal family relationships. It recognizes the roles and responsibilities associated with these connections, such as being a parent, sibling, or child. This view emphasizes the importance of our immediate and extended family members in our lives and acknowledges the legal and societal obligations that come with these relationships.

In simpler terms, the physical view tells us that our next of kin includes our family members by blood, marriage, or legal ties. These are the people who are related to us through birth or recognized by law as part of our family. They play significant roles in our lives, such as providing support, care, and companionship.

Understanding the difference between the spiritual and physical views allows us to see that while our biological or legal family is important, there is also a deeper spiritual dimension to our next of kin relationships. It reminds us that our connection to God and fellow believers is equally significant and can bring us a sense of belonging and support beyond what our physical family can provide.

By recognizing and honoring both perspectives, we can navigate the complexities of family dynamics, cherish our physical family ties, and cultivate a deeper spiritual kinship with God and our spiritual family. This understanding helps us appreciate the broader meaning and significance of next of kin relationships in our lives, fostering love, unity, and a sense of belonging in both our earthly and spiritual realms.

Remember, regardless of our level of understanding or background, the key message is that next of kin relationships encompass both the physical and spiritual aspects. It's about valuing and nurturing our biological or legal family ties while also recognizing and embracing our connection to God and fellow believers in the larger spiritual family.

In this chapter, we explored the concept of next of kin from both a spiritual and physical perspective. The spiritual view emphasizes our connection with God and fellow believers, transcending biological or legal relationships. It highlights the spiritual unity and shared identity we have as children of God. On the other hand, the physical view focuses on our biological or legal family ties, recognizing the roles and responsibilities associated with these relationships.

We discovered that understanding both perspectives is crucial for a holistic understanding of next of kin relationships. While the physical view addresses our earthly responsibilities and relationships, the spiritual view reminds us of the deeper spiritual bond we share as believers. Balancing these views allows us to navigate the complexities of family dynamics while recognizing the profound spiritual dimension of our next of kin relationships.

next of kin relationships are multi-faceted, encompassing both the spiritual and physical dimensions. Our spiritual view reminds us of our connection with God and the wider spiritual family, while the physical view acknowledges the importance of our biological or legal family ties. Both perspectives hold significance in shaping our understanding of familial relationships.

By embracing both the spiritual and physical views, we can foster deeper connections with our immediate and extended family members, as well as cultivate a sense of belonging within the larger spiritual family. Recognizing the importance of both dimensions allows us to appreciate the love, unity, and support that can be found within our next of kin relationships.

Ultimately, the concept of next of kin extends beyond biological or legal ties. It encompasses the spiritual unity we share as believers, regardless of our earthly relationships. By valuing and nurturing both the spiritual and physical aspects of next of kin connections, we can create a foundation of love, unity, and harmony that resonates with the timeless teachings of the Bible and enriches our lives in profound ways.

> Sarah and Rebecca: Sarah and Rebecca are childhood friends who have grown up together and share a deep bond. They have supported each other through various life challenges, celebrated each other's successes, and have become like sisters. Although they are not related by blood or legal ties, their unwavering support, love, and shared values make them each other's chosen next of kin.
> The Foster Family: Mark and Lisa have opened their hearts and home to foster children. They provide a safe and nurturing environment for children who have experienced difficult circumstances. Over time, they have developed strong bonds with these children, becoming their next of kin in a loving and supportive family setting.

These examples demonstrate that next of kin relationships can extend beyond traditional definitions. They showcase the power of love, commitment, and shared experiences in forming deep connections that transcend biological or legal ties.

As we conclude this book, it is important to remember that next of kin relationships are not solely defined by societal norms or legal frameworks. They are shaped by the love, care, and support we offer one another, whether through biological connections, chosen families, or spiritual bonds.

By embracing the spiritual and physical dimensions of next of kin, we can navigate the complexities of family dynamics, honor our familial responsibilities, and foster unity and harmony within our relationships. The timeless wisdom found in the scriptures, such as the examples of Ruth and Naomi, David and Jonathan, and the teachings of Jesus, serve as reminders of the importance of love, compassion, and support in our next of kin relationships.

May this book inspire you to reflect on the significance of next of kin connections in your life, encourage you to nurture and strengthen these relationships, and ultimately lead you to a deeper understanding of the love and unity that can be experienced within the next of kin bond.

As you continue on your journey, may you find solace, joy, and fulfillment in the embrace of your next of kin, both in the physical realm and the spiritual realm, knowing that through these connections, you are supported, cherished, and part of something greater than yourself.

Remember, in the tapestry of life, our next of kin relationships form the threads that weave a rich and beautiful story of love, belonging, and togetherness. Embrace the power of these connections and may they bring you lasting happiness, strength, and fulfillment.

Printed in Dunstable, United Kingdom